God's People, Pets, Poems and Sobriety

Lesette Schultz

Author's Tranquility Press
ATLANTA, GEORGIA

Copyright © 2023 by Lesette Schultz

All rights reserved. No part of this publication may be reproduced, distributed or transmitted in any form or by any means, including photocopying, recording, or other electronic or mechanical methods, without the prior written permission of the publisher, except in the case of brief quotations embodied in critical reviews and certain other noncommercial uses permitted by copyright law. For permission requests, write to the publisher, addressed "Attention: Permissions Coordinator," at the address below.

Lesette Schultz /Author's Tranquility Press
3800 Camp Creek Parkway, SW building 1400-116, #1255
Atlanta, GA 30331
www.authorstranquilitypress.com

This is a work of fiction.

Gods People, Pets, Poems and Sobriety/Lesette Schultz
Paperback: 978-1-960675-79-8
eBook: 978-1-960675-80-4

Contents

A girl Tammy and a family to me 3

Still learning to love.. 6

My Mom 8

My Mom 9

Kearney Street in Springfield Mo. 10

Judging People by color 12

Why do some not have much love in their families? 14

My Twin Sister 15

My Grandma Edna 17

Gifts from God 19

Deara, my Minx Cat 21

Happy the mother cat next door 23

Beautiful things everywhere 25

Always different things to do 26

Show Kindness to everyone 27

Gods People, Pets, Poems and Sobriety

A Family to me and their friends Tammy

I met a girl named Tammy twenty years ago through a family I had stayed with years ago. They were the Garrason's. Linda adopted her three grandchildren, she had every already when I moved in, she was three years old. About a year later, Linda and I picked up another one of her grandchildren named Verny from Saint John's hospital here in Springfield Missouri. He was three days old and not long after that Linda had gotten married to Dennis Goodman. After a little while, Linda and her mother went and got another one of her grandsons in Kansas City, Missouri. His name is James, he was two years old. We all delivered Penny Powers and put them on people's porches. We had so much fun, and we all went out together to eat together, we barbecued also. They had a big front yard with a circle drive. Then we sat outside, played frisbee and ball with the children. We had a lot of fun. Linda and I took turns cooking and I cleaned the house, and she did all the laundry.

It was an old house, but I loved it there because there was so much love and happiness there, in that old house with that family there and you could feel the real love and care for one another every day. Tammy, the girl that I had met through the family, dated Linda's son, Walter. Linda had two other sons, John and James. They were the dads of Linda's grandchildren. I did not see Tammy for years until one day I was outside of my apartment on college street, she walked up to me and asked if I recognized her. I said no, she said it's Tammy Linda's friend, then I recognized her. She has had a lot of struggles all of her life from day to day and I realized how I was and felt better. Then her and couldn't imagine what she was going through. Tammy asked if I had seen her husband and I told her no because I had never met him. You just never know what People are going through so we should try to understand them and help them because one day we might need someone to be there for us.

I cannot believe how cruel people can be to another person. I told those women that laughed at Tammy that they should not have laughed at her because she does not know or even understand the things that she says. I am so glad that I had met Tammy and when God does come he will take her to be with him because she has a sweet heart and cares about things in life, Tammy is a blessing she has taught me a big lesson in life and I am very glad God let me see what some people are going through in life, I thought I had it bad but I didn't and not as bad as she has. It is good to love people as they are like God says God is Love.

I listened to Tammy and she told me that her husband's girlfriend slammed Tammy's arm in the door when Tammy had caught her husband in bed with her, I asked why she did not leave him? She said because we have two children together one is nine months old and the other is eleven months old, two of my neighbors were next to us listening, they laughed at her like they laughed at me not even ten minutes earlier. Tammy was hurt and upset she wanted to leave right away, I stopped her told her to give me a hug goodbye and that I would pray for her and her husband. God tells us to watch who you go around because it can rub off on you and you can pick up their habits if you are around them and I don't want to be like that I want to be good to people, God wants you to love people as they are God is love. Tammy has done better after I had seen her a year later, she has improved a lot and it is a big

Miracle from God she met a man named Danny they are going to church together and love each other very much, it's amazing what God's love can do in someone's life and it's so wonderful! God is so good.

Still learning to love

I never knew what real love was. My Dad left my mom when I was three years old, he drank alcohol everyday and he also abused my mom. My mom was too busy to talk or to listen, she had two jobs and had to raise five children herself. I did watch my mom cook, she made very good meals, cakes and cookies to.

My twin sister had lost her arm so that was devastating to my mom, too.

I know mom does love and care about me now because she listens and talks to me now.

I am beginning to heal now, there was such a deep wound that I had that you couldn't comprehend. Now the hurt inside is almost completely gone and I am almost healed completely because of her love and caring for me now. There were so many times I felt empty years ago because my husband did not even care about me and did not know how to love me.

Could this of been a pattern, when my Dad did not show any love for my mom? I thought could it have been because of me somehow? But no, it was not because of me, they themselves were not taught to love, someone might have not talked or listened to them either, through the years.

When I truly got saved and I lost everything in my life, that's when I truly started to know what love was, the kind of true love God has for all of us, there is no deeper love than his, he will love you when all others are gone, he will care for you and understands you and always will. He will always be there, you cannot see him, but he is there.

It's like when someone you love leaves life, it's like they are still right there, beside you everywhere, like yesterday they are still in your thoughts, the things they did, they are still there.

God's presence is everywhere, in the air that we breathe, the water that we drink and bathe in and everything that is here. He is in everything because he has made everything.

There is still love left in the world because of God's love. It is getting bad in the world, but God is still in people's hearts, that's what makes the world good, God's love in the world.

My Mom

My mom raised five children by herself. My dad left when I was three years old and it had to be God that gave mom the strength to keep going, or she would not have made it this far. My dad died of alcohol, I know throughout the years he was drinking everyday because when he picked us up for weekend's he drank all of the time. Mom forgave him for him abusing her and she got along with him whenever he was around for us. Mom's in her eighty's now and fairly healthy and still walking.

Mom had always had good-paying jobs through the years, we were never hungry and we always had clothes and shoes. Almost every weekend we had money to go to the roller skating rink just over the railroad tracks in Bradley Illinois, we also went to the Drive Inn Theater outside in Kankakee Illinois one city over, mom made popcorn, Kool-Aid and lemonade to bring. Some weekends we went to a roller rink in Coal City Illinois, sometimes on the way we would stop at the A. & W. root beer stand in Wilmington IL. One city before Coal City and got an ice cream cone or a root beer drink, we had a lot of fun.

Some night's we stayed home and watched TV mom would make popcorn, Kool-Aid and lemonade.

My Mom

We all moved to Missouri from Illinois because of better weather, we moved out to the country to Brighton Mo. We had a swimming pool, horses and chickens, I use to love going outside to feed the chickens and collect the fresh eggs in the morning.

Mom had finally met someone who cared about her, they danced so beautifully together, it was a match made from heaven. He worked at Cox South Hospital in Springfield Mo. working on machinery if it broke down. He also was a good mechanic when one of our cars broke down, he fixed them. He also taught my son Richard how to work on vehicles. Mom and he got married and were very happy. He found out he had cancer and he did not live for very long, he might have had it a long time, poor mom, they were so happy together. I am proud of Mom and the Lord is also and I am glad that I have had her in my life.

To a very special, strong mom. I love you mom. God bless you.

Kearney Street in Springfield MO.

When my sister and I still lived in Brighton MO. with mom and her husband, my sister and I would jump in my twin's silver van and cruise Kearney Street. You cannot do that now because now you get into trouble if you do. They had nice street car's dunes buggies and race cars, all of us met a lot of friends on Kearney, one night my twin and I were the only ones that came to town in her van, we had just turned the corner onto Kearney St. coming off of Kansas Expressway and right on the right hand side was a little Handy's food store, there was about twenty five to thirty people standing in a circle we got closer and there was a car with the back and front windshield busted out there was a man lying in the back seat, it looked like he was dead, there was also a man setting halfway up in the front seat of the car, they were hurt and bleeding bad, there was a tall big man beating another small man, the small man was hurt and could not defend himself, I asked the people just watching, isn't anyone going to help him? but no one would do anything. I walked up to the big, tall man and said stop it! He said what are you going to do about it? I said no stop! I got in front of him so he would not hit the small man again, he hit me hard and knocked me to the ground.

Boy that really hurt bad I felt it all through my body and in just one minute my eye was swollen shut and everyone scattered and took off. Thank God it was all over but the pain, the pain for them was still there and for my black eye, but the fear was gone for them.

All three men went to the hospital they went to St. John's.

Thank God no one died, if we wouldn't have stopped one of them might have died or two. The policemen asked if I wanted to press charges and I told them no because I was afraid of the man, he was heartless.

All of them made it through, God had his hands on them.

I urge everyone that read's this book don't do what I have done, I did not think that man was going to hit me and knock me down, I was hurt too. Just call 911 that would be the best thing to do. God was still there with me through it all. Thank you, God, for your protection.

Judging People by color

I used to be judgmental of all different kinds of People, probably because they were different, that was not good because God made everyone different and he loves all, we should to.

I remember living on Walnut Street in Springfield Mo. in an Apartment, this man came over as I was leaving, he asked me where my sister was? He told me that she told him that she would be at my apartment, I told him no she is not here and he got furious and mad, I was in the front of the apartment building and I was very afraid, he told me that he was going to take his steel bat and split my head open and split me in two, I could not believe what was going on and why this was happening, he raised the bat and I kept begging him not to do it and a women came running off the sidewalk and she grabbed the bat out of his hands! She yelled at him and told him to get out of here! She was an African Women and she saved my life. I remember helping and probably saving the three men on Kearney Street after that happened to me, God helped me also because of that probably. I don't remember her name but I told her that she could stay at my place anytime she wanted, she stayed three nights, I think she was afraid he was going to come back, she went to court with me to tell the Judge what she had seen but I was too afraid to press charges on him. On then on I have loved everyone just for the way that they just are no matter what. It's very weird how such a dangerous situation like that can have you Love everyone just the way that they are. God had her there at that right time and very moment and anyone else might not have helped me at all and I know God led me outside in front at the right time so that I would not be trapped inside and die. I am very grateful to that Women and I cannot believe she risked her life to save me, she was not afraid of him at all, I thank God for her and I hope her life is wonderful, that she is well and I hope to see her someday, she might read this someday. I love you and God bless you my African American Angel.

Why do some people not have much love in their families?

I don't understand why families don't love each other like they used to anymore and why are there so many family members left behind and heartbroken? Why don't they love each other anymore? And why is there so much hate for each other anymore? Why? Why do they argue and fight for no reason at all?

Why my Lord why? It's not like it used to be anymore, it's awful and sad. God wants families to love each other the way that they are, the way that God sees it should be.

It does not make any sense to me, so I don't fight or argue I just let them be.

I wish they can see what they are doing to the whole family by not caring or trying to understand one another anymore. Families should be there for one another because God puts families together in love he does not tear them apart. Where is the love of God in families anymore? It isn't like it used to be anymore.

My Twin Sister

We lived in Pectone Illinois on a farm and my sister and I missed the bus to go to school and the farmer was nice to let us put corn into the corn elevator, we were nine years old then. My sister kept picking corn off of the ground, I told her that there was plenty up here and she did not listen.

The farmer took off and I didn't know why? I tried to catch him but he left as fast as he could. He spoke Spanish so I couldn't understand what he was saying. I came back to the corn elevator and I didn't see my sister, then went into the house and looked everywhere, I could not find her, and I went back outside and went towards the barn and said are you in there? She said no I am over here I said where? She said I am over where we were, I looked and I could not believe it, I thought she was going to die so I kept talking to her so she would not be so afraid I looked up to the sky and prayed dear God please help her and let her live.

I did not want to scare her so I did not cry or even get sick but felt like it. I did not want to leave her either so I stayed right by her side, I don't know how long I sat there, God was there and made me strong. My brother Terry came outside and he got sick and ran into the house to get my mom. My mother ran out to the road, in front of cars and semie's she almost got hit, I ran to try to calm her down and told her that help was on the way, I got her out of the road. I think I blacked out because the next thing I remember is I was in the house on the couch and my Grandmother was sitting next to me.

We all stayed with my Grandma Edna my mom's mom. My Dad came down from Georgia and got a motel, he stayed until my sister got better, she was at the hospital in Chicago Illinois.

I don't know why but when I went to see her at the hospital I was very afraid to see her, I did not go back and did not see her until she come home I know it was very painful for her, everyday day she said they scrubbed her shoulder with alcohol so that infection would not set into her body she was so strong. Thank you, Lord, for letting her live. My big and strong Twin sister Lucia, I love you, my sister. God is so good.

My Grandma Edna

My mom's mom lived in Bradley Illinois and my Grandma's favorite church was called Grace Baptist Bible College the next city over into Kankakee Illinois, they train people to become ministers there now. Kankakee, Bradley and Bourbonnais, are all together and small cities. My twin sister and I was born at St. Mary's Hospital.

My other two sisters Luzanne and Laura were born on the same day but two years apart, that was good because when I and my twin would have our birthdays the same day they would also. Our birthday is on Dec 20th. Theirs is Jan 10th. Both of our Grandmother's lived only a few blocks away from each other, we lived right in the middle of both of them and we all lived in Bradley Illinois. My mom was the only one that supported us and we had a nice house with a swimming pool in the backyard, it was wonderful.

My Grandma Edna was a very strong and Godly woman, she did not talk much but she was very wise and read the bible everyday. No one wanted to go to church with her that much so I tried as much as I could.

I started to drink beer mom did not know, I was sixteen and I hoped that my Grandmother had forgiven me for bringing that beer into her house, I knew in my heart she had, she had God in her heart. I remember to this day her saying to me yelling give me that beer now! I had both of my hands around that can of beer and she used only one hand and got that can of beer out of both of my hands, I still cannot believe how much strength God had gave to her that day, God made her very strong.

I remember when we stayed with her a few years earlier when my sister was still in the hospital she used to make oatmeal cookies every two to three days. Grandpa used to put his feet on the end of the kitchen table and when we came into the kitchen he would say hi boys to me and my sister's, it was very funny. He had two nice old cars that did not run that good, but they were nice. I remember all of the families would get together at my Grandma's house on holidays, aunts, uncles, cousins nephews and nieces, and my aunt's and mom would help my Grandma cook, they also made cakes and cookies. Everyone had so much fun, and got along and you could feel the love there. My Godly and wonderful Grandma Edna. Thank you, Lord for my Grandma Edna.

Gifts from God

People have different assignments from God, they are gifts that God gives them, through their mouths to speak or to use their hands to pray. Assignments from God can be just to speak, or listen to people to help them along the way. Just doing little thing's for people are assignments that some people have. I like to pray for people and some of the people do get healed by God, some don't. I did not understand why God did not heal everyone that I prayed for but it was their time to go with the Lord to be with him. God's plans are not ours, his is different and better in the end. I did not know that on of my assignments was to pray for people's healings, I liked praying for them and two Preachers told me that that was one of my talents and gift from God, another is singing to the Lord, I thank God for his gifts. Some people have made me feel stupid around other people when I prayed for them, they looked at me really weird, like they were not going to be healed, and some said they doubted.

I do not know for sure but I feel if someone does not have a little faith when you pray for them, they might not get healed, maybe I will never know about this but I do know that God knows.

I did not know why I had lost everything in my life but now I do know why, I had to lose everything and come to the Lord completely so that he could make me a better person for everyone that I am around.

I was stubborn and have had a lot of heartaches in my life but my joy is full now and he has restored a lot of the things that I had lost. I quit drinking and smoking cigarettes in the same year in 2004. I went through an alcohol treatment center at Sigma House on Park Ave and Alcohol Court at the courthouse on Boonville Ave. in Springfield Mo. There were people that really cared for me. I was a bad alcoholic and I thought I was not an alcoholic at all but after treatment, for over four month's I knew I needed help.

The people that saved me from drinking and dying cared for me and I am grateful, I want to live and not die. All of these people were gifts from god to me, I did not know this for a while. I am also thankful to have had Judge Calvin Holden in my life, he saved my life and has let me want to live and I want to help other people as he does. He is very special. I love you all, thank you so much for helping me.

God bless you!

With love,

Lesette

Deara, my Minx Cat

Deara is now eleven years old and it started with her mother.

I just moved into a house on Warren Ave. in Springfield Mo. There was an orange tabby cat sitting on my porch, I started feeding her and she finally came into the house, I did not have a name for her, and I was not going to keep her because every time I sat down to eat, she would grab food out of my plate even after I fed her, she was a wild cat. I had her in the house for about three weeks and she was running back and forth all through the house and crazy, I did not know she was pregnant.

My back porch was a closed-in back porch and it was connected to my kitchen. I came into the kitchen to see where she was, she came up to the top step into the kitchen from the back porch and was dragging something behind her, I freaked out for almost a minute, the kitten's head was dragging on the floor, I laid the mother down and slowly pulled the kitten out, then I used my finger nail's to break open the sack around the kitten, I got a wet warm-wash rag and washed the little girl kitten off, she did not have a tail, I had thought she was just born without one, she had long legs and looked like a fawn, a baby dear.

I could not believe I helped her deliver a kitten, I know it was God that helped me because I could not have done that on my own and without God's help.

Prayer does work and a lot of miracles come from prayer.

The mother cat delivered two more kittens, they were males and they had tails just like their mother. I found out that the father cat was a minx I saw him in the neighborhood and he did not have a tail and had long legs like Deara, the girl kitten that I had kept. Deara loves baths, she lays in my arms and talks to me when I talk to her she talks a lot. She is afraid of people and hides. There are only two people she will come over to, my old neighbor across the street Earlean she is a nice Christian woman that always talked to Deara and Debbie another lady I know. My sweet little cat talker Deara. Thank Lord for my cat.

Happy the Mother Cat next door

A cat named Happy lived next door, the neighbors let her out or she got out and was outside all of the time and they did not let her back in, it was below zero several times. She is so beautiful! She is black and it looks like someone splashed orange paint all over her. Happy loved to climb all the way to the tree right in front of my apartment, she loved it so much. The neighbors fought all of the time, one night Happy had blood all over her side, it looked like someone stabbed her with something she had a whole in it, I washed it out with Peroxide and put antibiotic inside the whole she had in her for a while and it finally closed up and healed. About a month later the lady next door said her boyfriend went to jail and she had to get an order of protection so he could not go around her I'm glad she is okay. The neighbor told me she could not take care of Happy anymore because she had no money to feed her so I put a cat carrier outside in the winter, I wrapped some cloths around the whole little cat carrier and wrapped plastic around the cloths and cat carrier, put two warm towels inside where she could lay and put two big rocks on top of the carrier so that the plastic would stay wrapped around it, she loved that warm bed that I had made for her outside. I sensed that she was going to have her kittens soon so I made her stay in my apartment, I made a bed for her in my bedroom closet and put a thick blanket on the floor, I put her on top of the blanket inside the closet twice rubbed her belly and told her to have her babies right here, the second night she started to have her babies at 2: o'clock Am. I had to help her because she screamed real bad for almost five minutes she could not get it out so I had to help her it was stuck so I prayed real hard and I begged and asked God to please help me to help her he did. I had experience because I learned by myself to deliver my orange minx cat Deara. I had to help her deliver all four kitten's, one looked just like her and it was a girl the other was all black and it was a boy then there were two Siamese kitten's and one was a girl and the other one a boy.

The Siamese kittens looked just like the father cat across the street and he was blind. After they were weaned off of their mother Happy I called the Humane society so that I could get the kitten's and Happy adopted out, someone there told me that someone adopted all three kittens and about a week later someone got Happy the mother cat. Happy is such a good mother and such a sweet cat and I will miss her very much and remember her always, I hope she will be as happy as much as when I had her and they take good care of her because she went through so much. I Thank God that he let me take care of Happy and her babies to because it was so beautiful and wonderful.

Beautiful things everywhere

Look at the Bird's in the air, look at the trees everywhere, God is always near and look how wonderful all of the things that God has made everywhere, the different kinds of bird's and all of the different kinds of things and people also everywhere, you cannot see him but he is there and you can also feel his presence everywhere. He makes you good, he makes you kind, he wants you to Love everyone just the way that they are, what a wonderful and caring God we have of ours. Try to be kind to people and Love them as they are because life is so short and it moves so fast as we age, if you do this you will have such a peace in your soul that you will never outgrow and when things get bad look at all of the beautiful things all around you and don't be sad because everything could be worse , thank God for all of the good things that he has brought to you, God is so good.

Always different things to do

Don't let the beautiful and different things pass you by because there is always different things to do everyday where here on earth, everyday is not the same so enjoy your day's in different ways, God will help you enjoy each day and in each and every different special way. God bless you all.

Show Kindness to everyone

What beautiful trees God has made, oh! How the leaves dance up and down, they wave at us and everything that goes by, they jump up and down for joy, they tap dance in the sky, how the leaves on the branches are so high, oh! What beautiful things he has made.

Look at all of the beauty all around us, with everything enjoy.

Show love and kindness where ever you go, care for everyone because God is watching us and very near.

Thank you Lord for all you have given us I love you Lord so much.

Life is so short so try to live life everyday like it's our last day because we never know when God will take us home to be with him to stay.

There is so much beauty all around us so live your life to the fullest, from day and to each passing day.

Everyday try to be happy, thankful, trust God and obey, he will help you along the way each and everyday.

God has helped me in every way. It is getting better for me now because I trust him, and I am living the right way.

I hope you enjoyed this book. God bless you all.

With Love,

Lesette Schultz

SchultzLesette2@gmail.com

Lesette Schultz

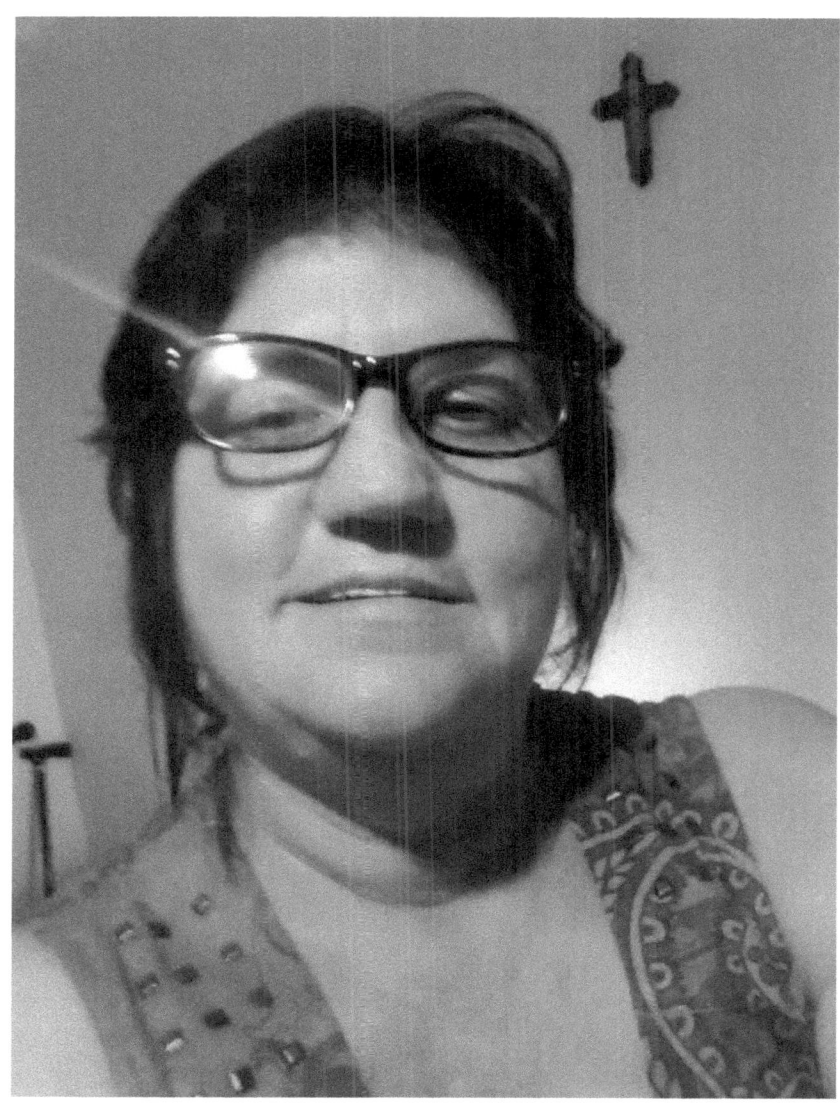

www.ingramcontent.com/pod-product-compliance
Lightning Source LLC
LaVergne TN
LVHW050027080526
838202LV00069B/6955